NEEDLEPOINTS TO GO

NEEDLEPOINTS TO GO

Small Projects for Spare Moments

by BRANDE ORMOND

HOUGHTON MIFFLIN COMPANY BOSTON

1975

Library of Congress Cataloging in Publication Data

Ormond, Brande.
Needlepoints to go.

1. Canvas embroidery.   I. Title.
TT778.C3075   746.4′4   75–6852
ISBN 0–395–20422–4

Printed in the United States of America

H   10   9   8   7   6   5   4   3   2   1

Dedicated to Billie Conkling

ACKNOWLEDGMENTS

I want to thank the many people who cheerfully worked samples for the photographs: Billie Conkling, Jane Cornbrooks, Bettina Dale, Ruthanne Dugan, Mom Smith, Judy Gordan, Barbara Green, Barbara Grové, Ginna Herrmann, Irene Kirilloff, Duddy Lally, Betty Lewison, Beka Martin, Betty McDonnell, Elaine Ormond, Kim Ormond, Ann Oster, Barbara Reed, Jane Rogers, Carol Smith, Frances Tenenbaum, Ted Theodore, and Ina Zoob.

I'm very grateful to Peggy Martin for her help and support during the writing of this book — also to my aunt, Ruthanne Dugan, Billy Martin, Arthur Mitchell, Libbie Nead, Carol Smith, and Jack Kohler for their help. I also want to thank Ann Oster for contributing her beautiful key ring design.

It is safe to say that there would be no book at all without the inexhaustible energy and enthusiasm of Beka Martin.

And very special thanks to my editor, Frances Tenenbaum, and copy editor, Linda Glick.

CONTENTS

THE DESIGNS

*Twelve color plates
precede The Designs*

NEEDLEPOINTS TO GO

INTRODUCTION

It is probably no accident that in our mechanized world many of us feel the need for a creative activity to express our own individuality of taste, of perception, of accomplishment. The number of weavers, backyard sculptors, and gardeners-in-season grows in proportion to the number of computerized communications we receive in every mail. And so does the number of needlepointers. In fact, one of the special virtues of needlepoint is that it is a portable hobby; you can do it any place and at any time — provided you have had the foresight to carry your bag of wool and canvas with you.

But sometimes even this isn't convenient or practical. An extra bag may be a nuisance on a plane. You didn't realize in advance that the doctor would keep you waiting an hour for your appointment. Perhaps the hostess will be offended if you arrive at her dinner party carrying a bag of work, so you leave it home and spend the evening sitting by in frustration while she and the other guests stitch contentedly away.

The answer, of course, is a little needlepoint project, small enough to carry in your pocket or purse "just in case," and quick enough to complete in spare moments, or even just as a change of pace between larger, more complicated needlepoint projects.

The demand for small needlepoints can easily be seen in the number of kits that have appeared on the market and in the number of little canvases that emerge from handbags as commuter trains pull out of the station.

Aside from the high cost of packaged kits, one wonders whether the end result is worth the effort. For some reason, small, quick needlepoints seem to be designed as picture exercises for beginners; the materials are usually coarse and the pictures trite.

But beginners can learn just as well, if not better, on projects that are both pleasing to work on and useful and beautiful when finished. Besides, even the most expert needleworker often wants to work on something small and quick. Although for the convenience of the reader I have labeled each of the projects in this book "Easy," "Intermediate," or "Advanced," I have tried not to compromise on the quality of any design, and an experienced needlepointer should be able to find pleasure in working even a so-called "Easy" project.

TRANSFERRING THE DESIGNS TO CANVAS

Each of the objects in this book is drawn full size against a graph background that corresponds exactly to the canvas on which it is to be worked. In addition, there is a color photograph of each piece, along with a list of the colors used and the amount of wool needed.

To reproduce the object, you can either trace the drawing or you can use the graph to count stitches — with or without tracing an outline. Most of the pieces can be worked either way, but a few, particularly those in which the motifs are adaptations of oriental carpets, can only be done by the counted-stitch graph method.

TO PREPARE THE CANVAS

Measure the outline of your project with a ruler and add three inches to the overall dimensions. The canvas for a 4-inch x 4-inch coaster, for example, should be 7 inches x 7 inches. This allows for a 1½-inch border of unworked canvas on each side, for blocking and handling.

Cut your canvas to this size and bind the edges by folding masking tape over the cut edge. The tape will keep your canvas from unraveling and will protect the wool from rubbing against the rough canvas.

TO TRACE THE DRAWINGS

Materials:

    Tracing paper
    Pencil
    Black felt-tip marker with a fine point or
        a speedball pen with India ink
    Masking tape
    Kneaded eraser
    Small tubes of black and white acrylic paint
    # 1 sable water color brush

All of these materials are available in any art supply store. Be sure to get a brush that forms a neat point when you wet it or you will have trouble painting a thin line. A kneaded eraser is the only kind that works on needlepoint canvas.

The felt-tip marking pen is to be used on the tracing paper. Never use a marking pen on canvas. Even the ones that claim to be indelible aren't safe to use because the sizing on the canvas may prevent the ink from penetrating into the fibers, and when you block or wash your needlepoint, the ink will wash off into the embroidery.

An easy, completely safe way to mark a design on canvas is to mix black and white acrylic paint to a light gray. Add enough water to give the paint the consistency of light cream.

For small pieces, it is important to have an accurate outline. With a ruler, measure to find the center of the canvas and mark this lightly with a pencil (Fig. 1). From the center, measure the overall dimensions of your project and outline it with brush and paint (Fig. 2). If the outline has rounded corners, paint each stitch (where the threads of the canvas cross) on one of the curves (Fig. 3) and then

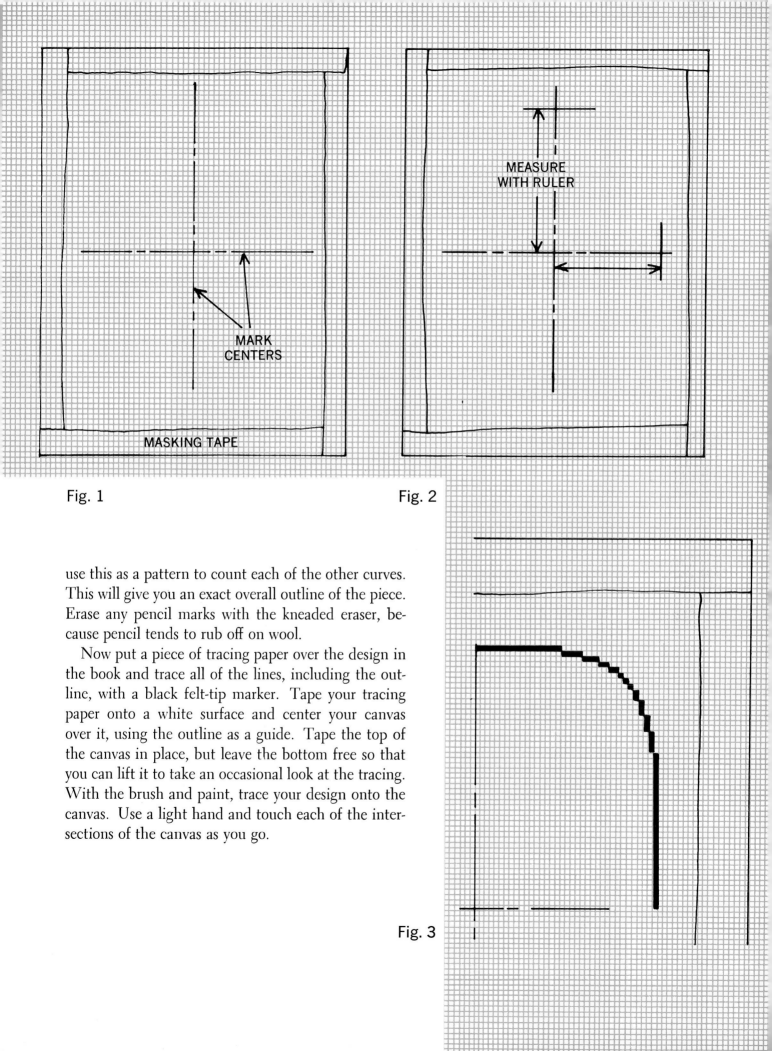

MARK CENTERS

MASKING TAPE

Fig. 1

MEASURE WITH RULER

Fig. 2

use this as a pattern to count each of the other curves. This will give you an exact overall outline of the piece. Erase any pencil marks with the kneaded eraser, because pencil tends to rub off on wool.

Now put a piece of tracing paper over the design in the book and trace all of the lines, including the outline, with a black felt-tip marker. Tape your tracing paper onto a white surface and center your canvas over it, using the outline as a guide. Tape the top of the canvas in place, but leave the bottom free so that you can lift it to take an occasional look at the tracing. With the brush and paint, trace your design onto the canvas. Use a light hand and touch each of the intersections of the canvas as you go.

Fig. 3

o LIGHT BROWN
x MEDIUM BROWN
■ DARK BROWN
. LIGHT GRAY
/ DARK GRAY

There are two ways to use the drawings as graphs. You can paint in the overall outline, as you did above, and then — instead of painting the lines of the design — simply count the stitches as a guide to where the colors go. The other kind of graph has symbols for the different colors. If you use this kind of a graph, you don't have to draw an outline of the entire piece, but do be sure to find the center of the canvas before you begin.

One virtue of the graph method is that it makes it very easy to enlarge or reduce the size of a finished piece. Thus, if you wanted to enlarge a key ring that is drawn on a #18 canvas, simply count the stitches onto a #14 or #10 canvas. On the other hand, if you want your finished object to come out to the exact size of the design in the book, be sure *not* to change the canvas size. (The various sizes of canvas are described in detail in the Materials section, p. 21).

USE OF COLOR

You may follow the color photographs and the lists of colors that accompany each drawing. Or you can change the colors completely. It is also possible, by using more or fewer colors, to achieve many different effects from one drawing. A leaf done in one shade of green will appear stylized and contemporary (and will also be easier to do, if you are a beginner). The same leaf done in seven shades of green will be more realistic. Wherever possible, the names of the animals, flowers, and shells are given, so that you may look them up in field guides if you want to reproduce them faithfully.

If colors don't look right to you, don't hesitate to make substitutions. It is often difficult to predict how one color will look next to another or against a different background. A color that looks bright against a light background may seem dim against a very dark one.

Experiment with colors. Most people assume that different shades of the same color must be taken from the same family — four shades of purplish blue, for example. This is always safe and tasteful, but it is also boring. You will get more vibrant and interesting effects by using shades from different families.

The more color, the better. Since many of these pieces call for one or two strands of a color, try substitutes from your leftovers; it's a good way to stretch your mind and your budget. If you force yourself to experiment, you will become more open about color. Most people have at least a few color prejudices, but even if you think you loathe pink, you may find it essential for a certain shell or flower.

The one color you should avoid is black, which tends to look too severe, as if the canvas had a hole burned in it. If you think you are seeing black, substitute a very dark brown, or blue, or gray, or some other appropriate color. There are two exceptions to this rule in this collection — the stuffed-toy skunk and the keyhole in one of the key ring designs both call for black.

MATERIALS

Please use the very best wool and canvas you can buy. On small pieces the difference in cost between good materials and those of inferior quality amounts to mere pennies. There is a great deal of difference, though, in the appearance and durability of the final object, as well as the pleasure you will get in working with fine wool and canvas.

WOOL

The wool I recommend is Paternayan Persian yarn. It comes in more than 400 colors, has a beautiful silky texture, and yet, because of its especially long fibers, is extremely tough — it was originally made to repair Persian carpets — and is available at most needlepoint shops.

Persian yarn has another distinct advantage over other wools. Since it is a three-thread yarn, it is adaptable to canvases of varying sizes. For the patterns in this book, use the full three-thread strand for #10 canvas; two threads for #14 canvas, and a single thread for #18 canvas.

Generally, Persian yarn is sold by the strand. Each strand is approximately 33 inches long. The quantities of yarn needed for these pieces are given in those terms, and the number of 33-inch strands required appears after each color. Some stores, however, now carry Persian yarn in small packaged hanks (usually 10 yards) instead of individual strands, which means that you may sometimes have to buy more than you will actually need. Don't be concerned about this; it's a good way to build up your source of yarn for other projects, just as these needlepoints are a good way to use up yarn you already have on hand.

If you prefer to use tapestry yarn, or have some around, be sure to test it on your canvas before you start work. It should slide easily through the holes but cover the threads of the canvas completely.

Don't use leftover knitting or crochet wool. It doesn't have the long fibers of Persian or tapestry yarn and will "pill," wear out, or even break as you use it.

CANVAS

Canvas comes in single-thread weave (mono) or double weave (penelope). The instructions and thread-counts in this book are given for mono canvas, which most people find easier to work. If you are accustomed to penelope canvas, there is no reason why you can't use it, but check to be sure you are using the correct number of threads of wool to cover the canvas.

Canvas is numbered according to how many holes there are to the inch. The pieces in this book are limited to three sizes of mono canvas — #10, #14, and #18. Obviously, #10 canvas is the fastest and usually easiest to work, #18 the slowest and finest. Since #10 worked canvas is heavy for very small pieces, and #18 too painstaking for some people, the majority of the articles in this book call for #14, which works out to be a very good compromise.

Like fabric, canvas is sold by the yard, in widths usually of 36 inches. For the most part, one piece of canvas of whatever length you need will provide you with material for several projects. (It is only when you start buying your own wool and canvas that you realize how inexpensive beautiful needlepoint can be!)

The best quality of canvas comes from France and West Germany. It has a firm, even twist that is smooth to the touch. Cheap canvas is rough, and has a lot of sizing to make it appear shiny. Heavily sized, rough canvas is hard on your hands and your wool.

Don't accept *any* canvas that has a flaw or a bump. It will show up in your finished work.

NEEDLES

You should use blunt-ended tapestry needles, *not* sharp embroidery or sewing needles. Tapestry needles come in many sizes, and as long as the wool slips into the eye of the needle and the needle goes through the canvas easily, any size you are comfortable with is all right. The recommended sizes are a #18 needle for #10 canvas; #20 needle for #14 canvas, and #22 needle for #18 canvas.

Canvas gauge	Threads of Persian yarn	Needle size
#10	three (full three-thread strand)	#18
#14	two	#20
#18	one	#22

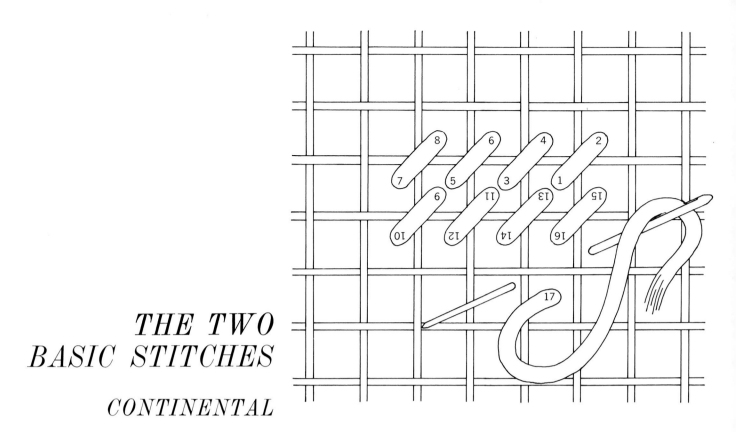

THE TWO BASIC STITCHES

CONTINENTAL

The continental stitch is used for the design portion of the canvas and as an outlining stitch. You can use it for the whole piece, although where there is a lot of background you will probably find that the basketweave stitch goes faster and doesn't pull your canvas out of shape, thus making it easier to block the finished work.

Begin at the top right of the area to be covered.

1. Bring the needle up through the hole at point #1.

2. In one motion, pass it into the hole to the diagonal upper right, then across two vertical canvas threads in the back, and up through hole #2. This is the beginning of the second stitch. Continue this way to the end of the row, drawing the needle to the back of the work to complete the last stitch.

3. To begin the next row, turn the canvas completely upside down, so that you will again be working from right to left.

4. Pass the needle up through the hole at point #9 and proceed as above.

BASKETWEAVE

The basketweave stitch is faster than the continental because the canvas is not turned for each row but is held stationary as you work in rows up and down on the diagonal.

Begin at the top right of the area to be covered.

1. Bring the needle up through the hole at point #1 and pass it into the hole to the diagonal upper right (#2).
2. Come up through the hole at point #3, and in one motion put your needle into the diagonal upper right hole (#4), then straight under two canvas threads vertically, and come up through the hole at point #5.
3. Pass the needle into the diagonal upper right and up through the hole at point #6.
4. Continue, following the numbers on the diagram, noting that the needle is in a horizontal position as you work a row going up and in a vertical position coming down.
5. Be careful not to stop work at the end of a row, because you will not know which way the next row goes, and two rows worked in the same direction will cause a noticeable ridge. To prevent this, always stop in the middle of a row and leave the threaded needle in the canvas aimed the right way.

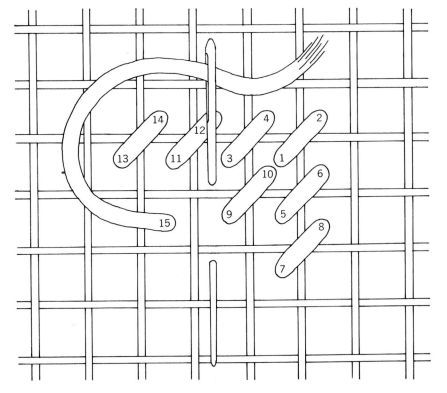

BLOCKING

If your piece is not soiled or out of shape, simply freshen it with a light steaming. Lay the embroidery, face down, on the ironing board and steam the wrong side. Don't use too much pressure or you will flatten the stitches, and never iron the right side or the stitches will be flat and shiny.

If your needlepoint is soiled or pulled out of shape, it must be washed — which is why it is so important never to risk using any paint or marker that might run when wet. Remove the masking tape and run several rows of machine stitching around the edges of the canvas to prevent the threads from unraveling during blocking. Then wash gently in cold or lukewarm water with a detergent made for woolens. Never rub or squeeze. After rinsing, roll the canvas in a towel and blot away excess water.

Cover a bread board or a cutting board with a clean white sheet. Use tracing paper and pencil and trace the outline of the piece from the book. Lay the paper containing the outline on the board and the damp needlepoint over it. Put two or three tacks in the canvas border at the top (*never* in the embroidered part), lining up the edge of the worked area to match the outline beneath. Follow the tracing around the entire edge, tacking as you go, until the embroidery is in its original shape. Put the tacks close together to keep the edges straight, but hammer them in just enough to hold, or you'll have trouble getting them out. Let the piece dry thoroughly before you remove it from the board.

Don't use spray soil repellents on needlepoint: the sprays tend to rough up the fibers of the wool and have been known to cause even waterproof paints to run.

FINISHING

Within the past year, at least two books have been published devoted exclusively to finishing needlepoint pieces. If this seems like a very specialized subject for a whole book, it also indicates a clear need for that kind of information. It is discouraging, to say the least, to put a lot of time and love into a needlepoint work and then discover that it costs a small fortune to have it finished professionally — if you are lucky enough even to locate a professional finisher.

For this reason, you will find complete directions for finishing every article in this book, immediately following the design. By putting the finishing instructions with the patterns instead of at the back of the book, the location to which they are usually relegated (or brushed off), you can take the problems of finishing into consideration when you select your project. In fact, the sequence of the designs is based upon the ease or difficulty of finishing. The patches and the coasters are the easiest; the picture frames the most challenging.

Although I design needlepoint, teach others how to do it, and love to needlepoint myself, in the past I have always had my work finished professionally. For this book, though, I personally finished every one of the articles in the photographs. I did this purposely, so that I could understand and explain to other amateurs like myself exactly what problems they might meet and how to overcome them. In the process, I discovered that finishing isn't nearly as difficult as I had thought! Some pieces can be finished entirely by hand. In other cases, you need a sewing machine or a friend who has one.

Like everything else, this work has its own lingo. Here are some terms you'll want to know:

Right side — the side of embroidery or fabric that will be facing out when finished. In the diagrams, the right side is shaded in gray.

Wrong side — the back of embroidery or fabric, the side that will not be visible when finished.

Bias — a line that is at a 45° angle to the grain of the fabric.

Gusset — the narrow piece of embroidery or fabric sewn between two sides to create a space between them. Gussets are used for the bottoms and sides of the tote bags in this book.

Seam allowance — the fabric between the cut edge and the seam, usually ½ inch.

Cording — string or cord that is covered with fabric and then sewn into the seams.

THE PLATES

4

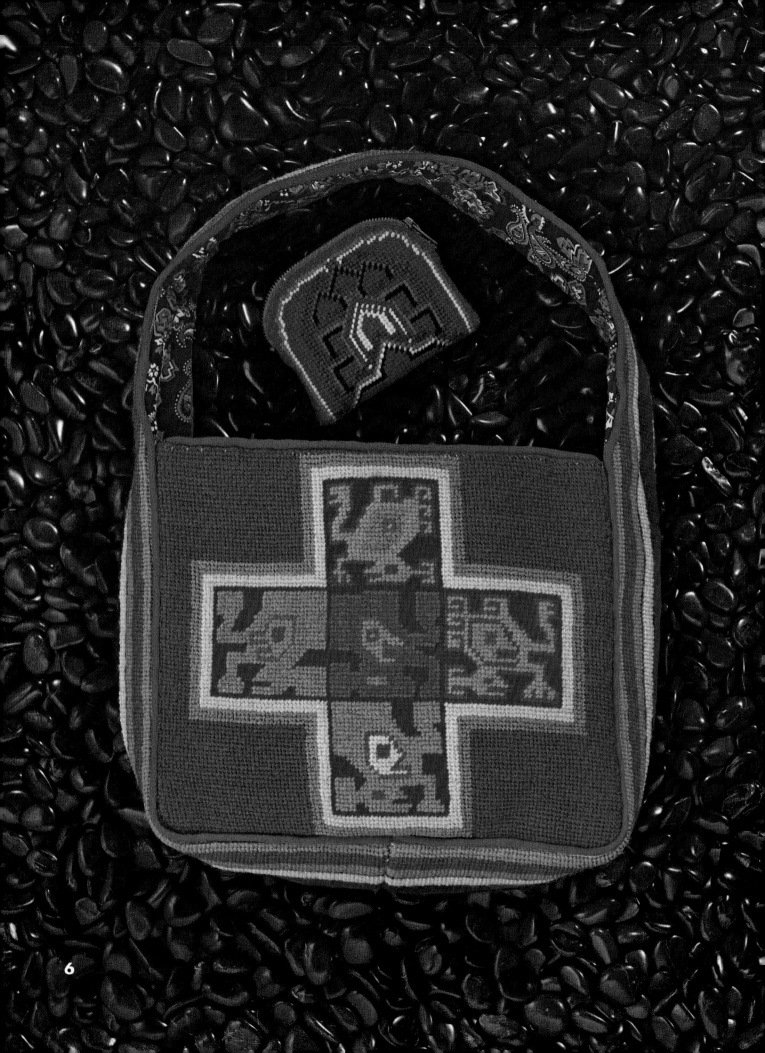

THE DESIGNS

PATCHES

Needlepoint patches are the smallest, simplest projects in this book — and among the most versatile. Use them to cover holes or decorate jeans and jackets; turn them into pockets; add a few extra rows of stitches and make them into coasters. Or use them for pillow centers. Keep in mind that almost any 3-inch square of the designs in this book can be made into a patch.

Patches should be worked on #14 or #18 canvas — #10 is too bulky.

The numbers following each color refer to the number of *full* 33-inch strands of wool you need to complete the patches in the color photographs. The number of threads of wool depends on the gauge of the canvas.

Orange	3
Blue	1
Red	2
Magenta	2
Background	9

(Plate 1)

Peruvian Cat

(Easy)

#14 Canvas. Two threads of wool.

This design is adapted from a tapestry woven in Peru about 600 years ago.

33

(Plate 1)

Cucumber Beetle

(Intermediate)

#18 Canvas. One thread of wool.

This creature appears in the color photographs as a patch, but if you want to make a pair of pillows it would be a nice mate to the Luna Moth on the next page.

Light gray	1	Medium green	1
Dark gray	1	Dark green	1
White	1	Background	6
Light green	1		

(Plate 10)

Luna Moth

(Easy)

#18 Canvas. One thread of wool.

Luna moths are actually a luminous green, so find a pale yellow green that seems to glow.

Light green	3	Beige	1
Dark green	1	Medium beige	1
Orange	2	Background	6
Sienna	1		

(Plate 1)

Indian Patch

(Easy)

#18 Canvas. One thread of wool.

A very simple design from a Shiraz Kilim (Persian) carpet can be a nice color study. Try doing several in different color combinations.

Light blue	3
Dark blue	1
White	2
Red	4
Dark red	1

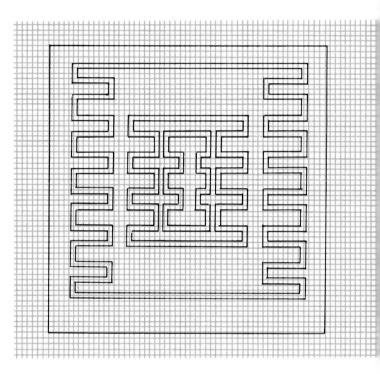

FINISHING PATCHES

1. Turn raw edges to the wrong side and baste.
2. Pin the patch to the garment and sew by hand with invisible stitches. You could also use the zigzag setting of a sewing machine and satin-stitch around the edges.

FINISHING PATCH PILLOWS

Materials:
    String for cording, any kind.
    Pillow material: ½ yard of any sturdy non-stretch fabric
      such as velvet, corduroy, faille, or wool.
    Muslin for inner pillow.
    Filling: cotton, kapok, dacron, or feathers.

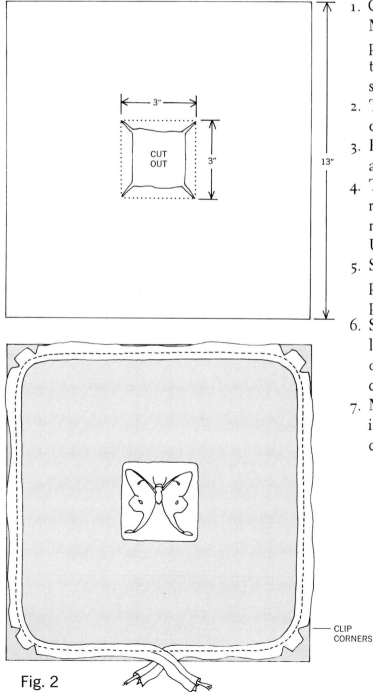

Fig. 1

Fig. 2

CLIP
CORNERS

1. Cut two 13-inch squares of backing material. Measure a 3-inch square in the center of one piece with a ruler, mark it with chalk, and cut out the center of this area, clipping to corners, as shown in Fig. 1.

2. Turn the edges to the wrong side and baste them down.

3. Place the patch behind this hole, pin it in place and sew it with invisible stitches, by hand.

4. To make cording, cut a piece of the pillow material 1½ inches x 45 inches on the bias. Fold it, right sides out, over the string, and sew closed. Use the zipper foot of your machine for this.

5. Sew the cording around the right side of the front piece (Fig. 2). Round the corners to prevent pulling.

6. Sew the front and back with right sides together, leaving 8 inches open at one edge. Check frequently to see that your stitches are close to the cording. Turn the pillow right side out.

7. Make an inner pillow of muslin, 14 inches x 14 inches and stuff it. Place it inside the needlepoint cover and sew the open edge closed by hand.

COASTERS

Needlepoint coasters are not only beautiful, they are also practical. Rubberized backing material makes them waterproof, and the needlepoint wool absorbs moisture from the glass, which is more than you can say for most coasters. Like patches, the coaster designs can be used as centers for fabric pillows; or you could enlarge the background and make them into all-needlepoint pillows. To use other designs in this book for coasters, simply trace the design onto a 4-inch square.

(Plate 5)

Seashell Coasters

(Intermediate)

#14 Canvas. Two threads of wool.

The shells in these four coasters should be shaded carefully with soft colors and the same background should be used for the set. If you look at the color photograph, you will notice that each of the shells throws a shadow against the background. To outline the shadow, move the canvas ¼ inch to the left after the design has been counted or traced, and trace the outline where the shadow falls. Stitch this area in a slightly darker shade of the background color.

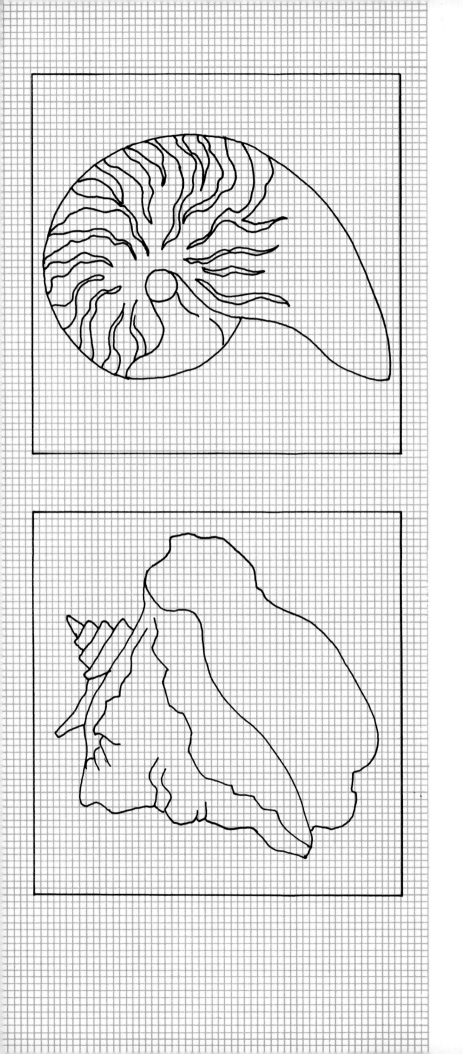

Nautilus

Light gray	1
Dark gray	1
Grayish white	1
White	2
Pale ivory	2
Ivory	2
Light tan	3
Tan	3
Light rust	1
Dark rust	1

Queen Conch

Medium brown	2
Tan	2
Dark yellow	2
Light yellow	2
Light pink	2
Pink	1
Peach	1
Light rose	1
Dark rose	1
White	2

Leopard Scallop

Light pink	4
Light lavender	3
Dark yellow	1
Medium brown	1
Dark rose	1

Magnificent Wentletrap

White	2
Pale gray	4
Medium gray	3
Dark gray	3

Background for all	60
Shadows for all	10

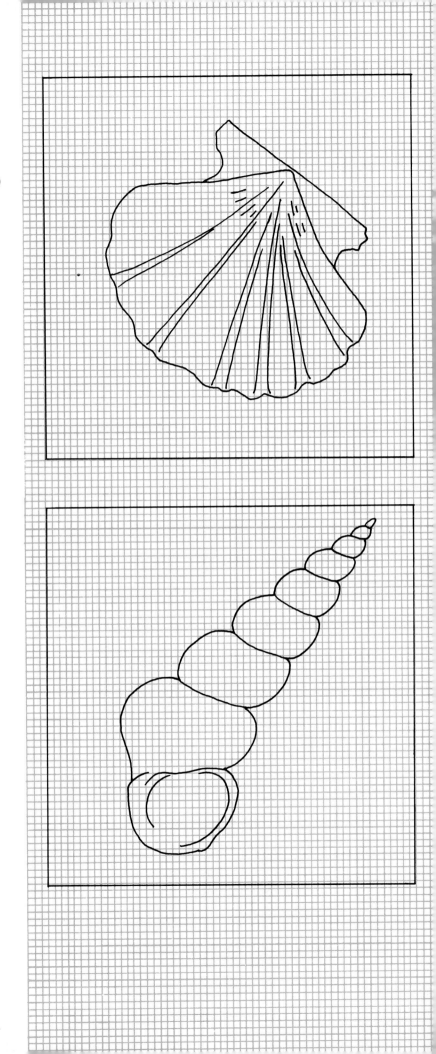

(Plate 7)

Wildflower Coasters

(Easy)

#14 Canvas. Two threads of wool.

Here is another set of four coasters which can be done as they are shown on plate 7, with simple shading, or worked in bright colors with no shading at all for a very contemporary effect.

Bellflowers

Light blue	2	Dark green	2
Dark blue	2	Yellow	1
Light green	3		

Thistle

Light green	4	Light purple	2
Medium green	2	Dark purple	2
Dark green	1		

Violets

Light green	3	Yellow	1
Medium green	4	Light purple	3
Dark green	2	Dark purple	2

Columbine

Light yellow	2	Medium green	3
Dark yellow	1	Dark green	2
Light green	4	Brown	1

Background for all 60

FINISHING

Materials:

Rubberized sheeting — available at department and fabric stores.

Heavy duty aluminum foil.

1. Run several rows of machine stitching ¼ inch from the edge of the worked area. Trim away excess canvas.
2. Fold the raw edges to the wrong side, mitering the corners, and baste by hand (Fig. 1).
3. Fold a piece of aluminum foil twice to form a 3½-inch square. Center this on the wrong side of the coaster. Pin it in place from the right side.
4. Cut a piece of rubberized sheeting 3¾ inches square and sew, by hand, to the back with small neat stitches (Fig. 2).

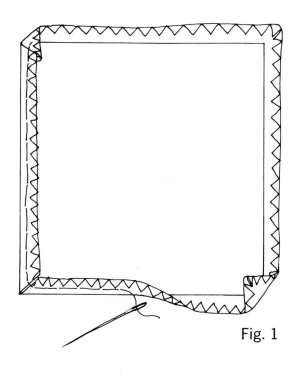

Fig. 1

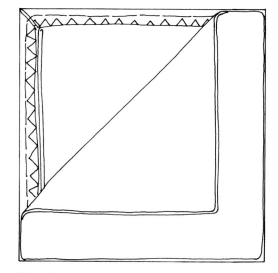

Fig. 2

HOT PADS

Here is another project that is simple and practical. The hot pads are washable and, like the coasters, lined with aluminum foil, which deflects the heat.

(Plate 2 and page 43)

Peas on a Vine
(*Easy*)

#14 Canvas. Two threads of wool.

Use two different colors of green for the pods and two for the foliage. Be sure to put a dot of white on each of the peas to make them shine.

White	1	Light yellow-green	5
Light green	2	Medium yellow-green	4
Medium green	2	Dark green	2
Dark green	1	Background	35

(Plate 2)

Radishes
(*Intermediate*)

#14 Canvas. Two threads of wool.

This one requires a little more shading than the peas, but is not difficult.

Light green	8	Medium pink	1
Medium green	4	Dark pink	1
Dark green	2	White	1
Red	1	Gray	1
Light pink	1	Background	30

FINISHING

Follow the directions for coasters, adjusting the size of the aluminum foil to 5½ inches square and the rubberized sheeting to 5¾ inches square.

KEY RINGS

Needlepoint is tough and will stand the punishment of daily use as a key ring. The ring with the monogram would also make a handsome luggage tag.

(Plate 11)

East Indian Flowers

(Intermediate)

#18 Canvas. Single thread of wool.

The flowers in this design are adapted from the decoration around a portrait of a lady done in the eighteenth century in India. (Use pinks for the flower not shown in the color plate.)

Light pink	1	Dark green	1
Medium pink	1	Orange	1
Darkest red	2	Dark orange	1
Gold	2	White	1
Light green	1	Background	10

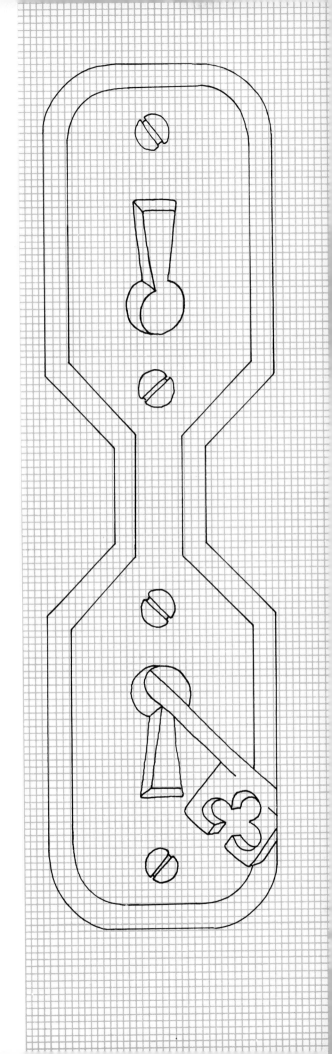

(Plate 8)

Keyhole

(Easy)

#14 Canvas. Two threads of wool.

This is one occasion when black yarn is appropriate, since you want to produce the illusion of a hole in the canvas.

Light yellow	1
Medium yellow	2
Dark yellow	1
Gold	2
Dark gold	1
Black	1
Background	24

(Plate 12)

Oriental Rug

Designed by Ann Oster
(Advanced)

#18 Canvas. Single thread of wool.

As you will notice, this key ring looks larger than the others. For the sake of clarity, it is shown on a #14 graph, but if you work it on a #18 canvas, it will be the same size as the other key rings in this series. Obviously this piece should be counted from the graph, not painted or traced. To make the reverse side, simply turn the book upside down to work the mirror image of the design. Or put a monogram on the back.

Actually, this design could be used in any number of ways, and on #10 or #14 canvas, too. It would

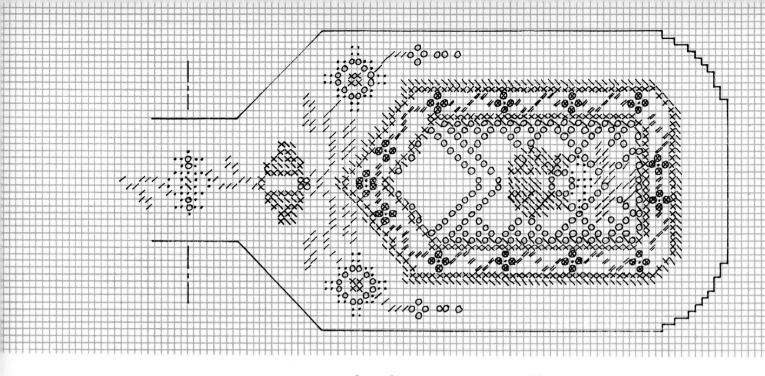

make a charming miniature wall hanging or a prayer rug for a doll's house.

Note that there are three separate backgrounds: the center, the border, and the outer edge.

Yellow	2	o		Light blue	2	x
Light green	1	//		Dark blue	2	\
Dark green	1	/		Lavender	1	⊗
Red	1	.				

Backgrounds:				
Beige	8		Dark red	4
			Royal blue	4

(Plate 8)

Monograms

(Easy)

#14 Canvas. Two threads of wool.

Place a piece of tracing paper over the initials you want and trace them so they overlap slightly. Cut a piece of canvas, draw the key ring outline on it, and place it over your tracing, making sure the monogram is centered. Now, with gray paint, transfer the monogram to the canvas. Or count stitches from the graph if you prefer, beginning with the center initial.

Green	2
Background	24

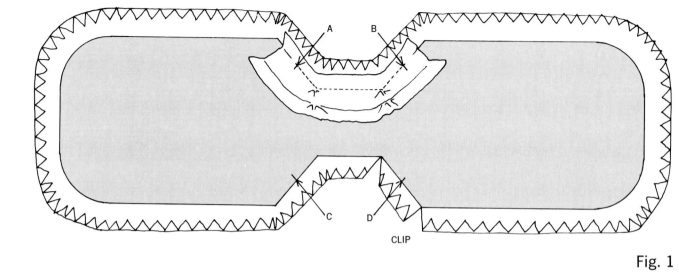

Fig. 1

FINISHING

Materials:

Key ring: split ring, ball chain, or spring sleeve, available in five-and-ten and hardware stores.

Four inches of cotton bias binding the same color as the background of the needlepoint.

Heavy interlining such as pelon or buckram.

1. Run several rows of machine stitching on the canvas border ⅜ inch from the worked area. Trim the canvas to this stitching.

2. Cut a piece of bias binding 2 inches long and sew it, right sides together, between points A and B in the dia-

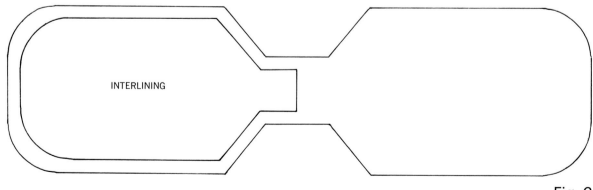

Fig. 2

gram (Fig. 1). Clip the corners as shown. Repeat this on the other side between C and D.

3. Cut a piece of interlining for one half and slightly smaller than outline, as shown. Lay it on one side of the wrong side of the needlepoint (Fig. 2).

4. Turn the raw canvas edges to the wrong side and baste, catching the interlining as you sew.

5. Fold the needlepoint over the key ring or chain, right sides out, and sew by hand around entire edge.

6. Take a piece of the same wool you used for the background and whipstitch over the seam, covering any bare canvas that might still show.

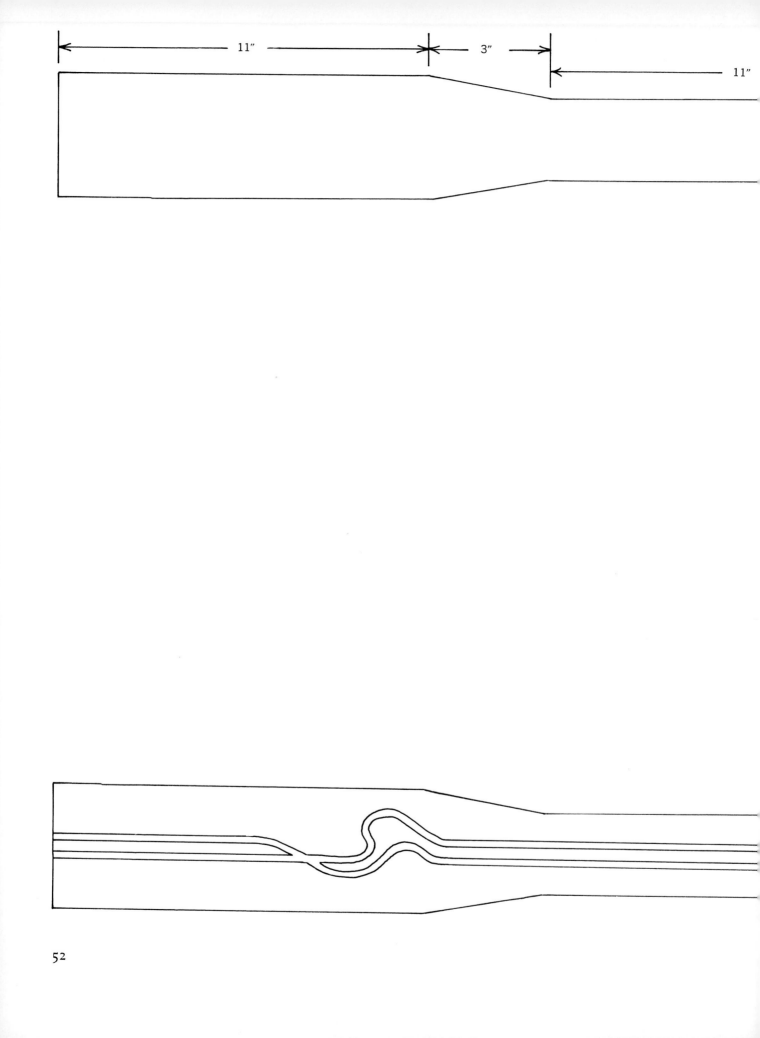

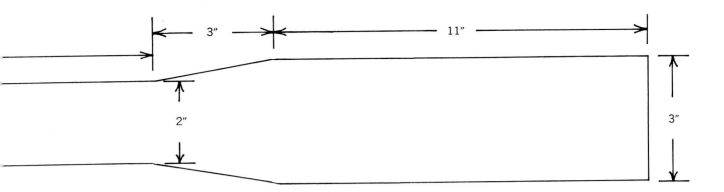

TOTE BAGS

Cut two pieces of canvas, one for each side of the bag. Be sure to leave a 1½-inch margin all around. Cut another piece, 42 inches x 6 inches, to make the gusset and handle. To draw the outline for the gusset, use the measurements on the diagram above.

(Plate 11)

Lily Tote

(Intermediate)

#14 Canvas. Two threads of wool.

The lilies of this piece come from a set of kneelers designed by the author for St. Mary's Chapel in the National Cathedral in Washington, D.C. It is the Madonna Lily.

To work the design on the gusset, make two tracings on paper from the portion of the design shown in

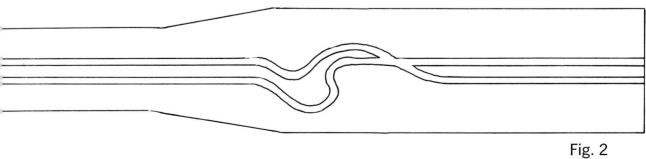

Fig. 2

Fig. 1. Put one tracing under one side of the canvas; turn the other one over and upside down and place it under the opposite side. Adjust these two so that when the two stems are continued up along the handle, they will meet in the center (Fig. 2). Now transfer them to the canvas.

White	20
Light gray	10
Dark gray	4
Yellow	4
Light green	40
Dark green	12

Backgrounds:

Light	90
Dark	125

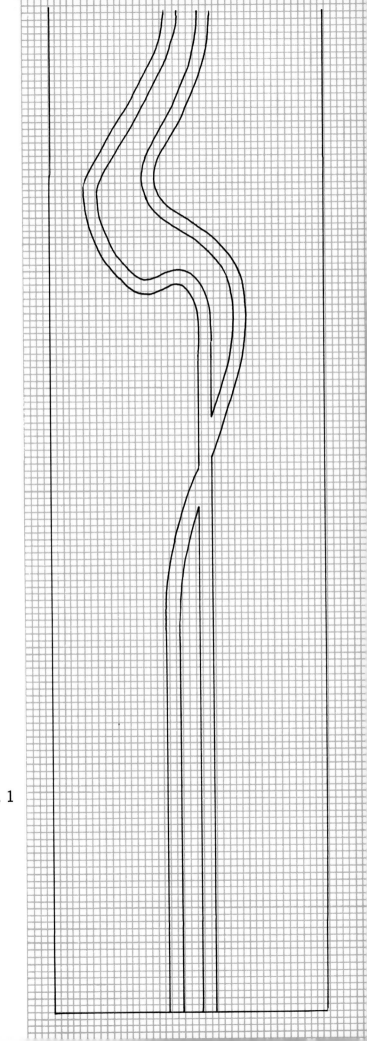

Fig. 1

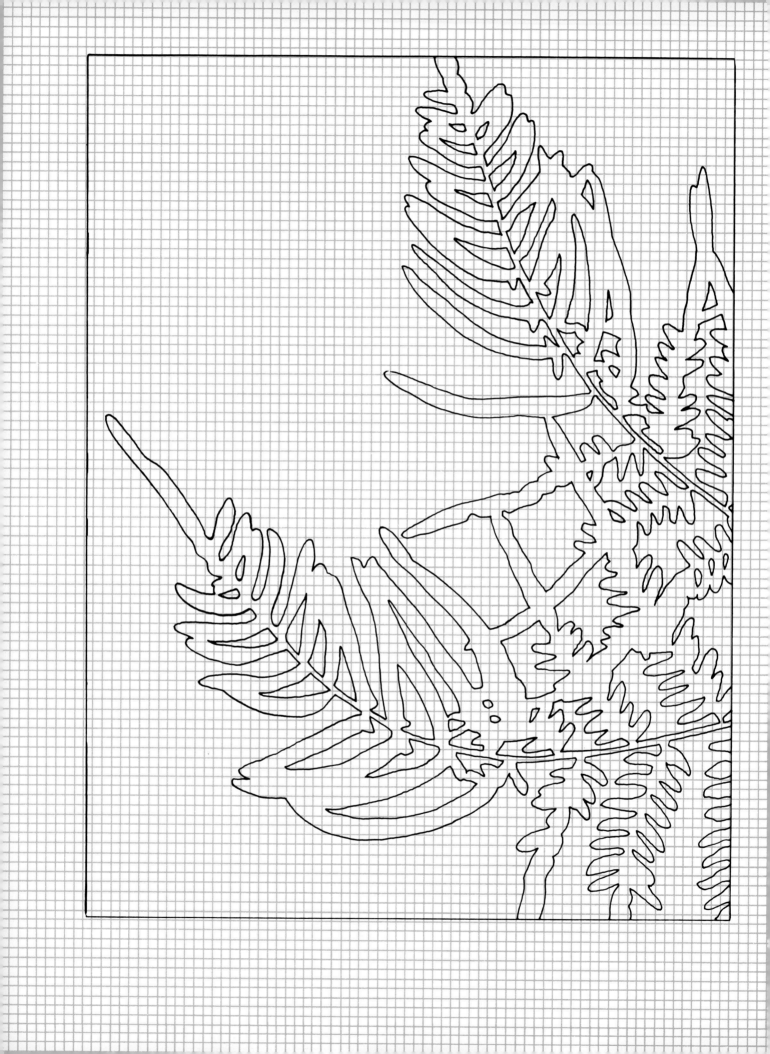

(Plate 9)

Fern Tote

(Easy)

#10 Canvas. Full strand of three-thread wool.

The fern on this tote is a common one. I first saw it in the woods of northern Florida. A simple design with only two colors, the complexity of the fern makes it delicate and pretty even on #10 canvas.

To work the design on the gusset, make a tracing on paper from the design in Fig. 3. Transfer it to one side of the canvas, turn it over and upside down for the opposite side, as in Fig. 1 (Lily Tote).

Green for design   120
Background   225

Fig. 3

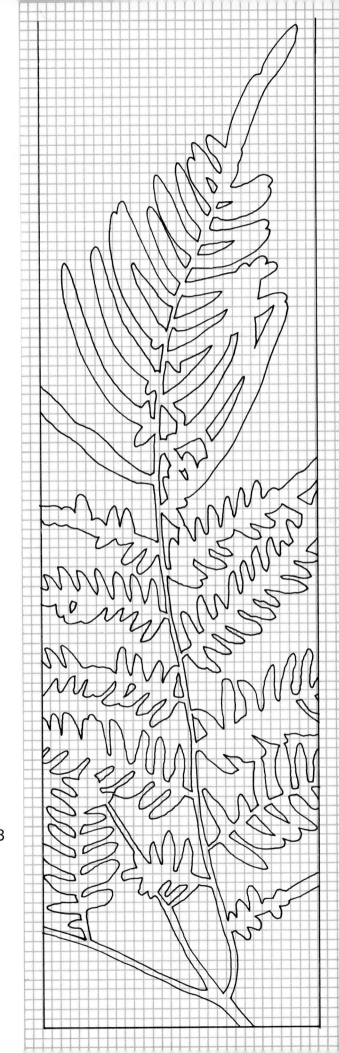

(Plate 6)

Peruvian Tote

(Easy)

#14 Canvas. Two threads of wool.

These abstract birds in a geometric shape come from a mantle woven in Peru during the Nazca-Wari period, somewhere around A.D. 100–700. Use bright colors, in combination with some earth colors to set them off.

To work the design on the gusset, simply count the rows of color from the graph.

Green	20	Sienna	14
Orange	37	Hot pink	26
Medium yellow	12	Light yellow	60
Dark brown	52	Tan	30
Red	28	Background	100

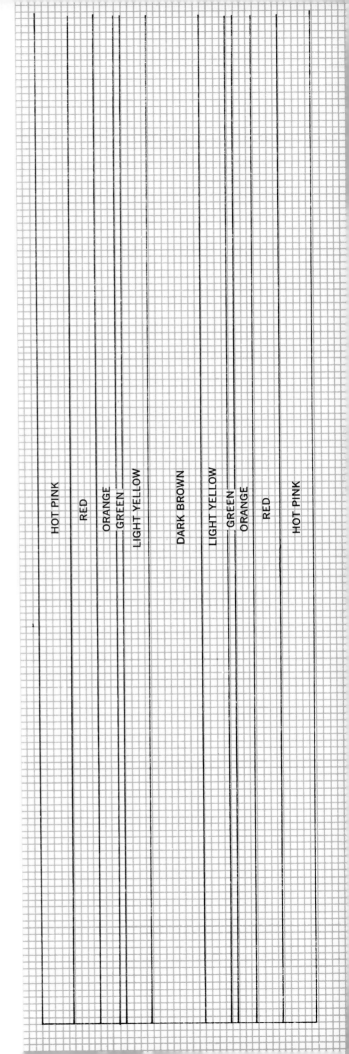

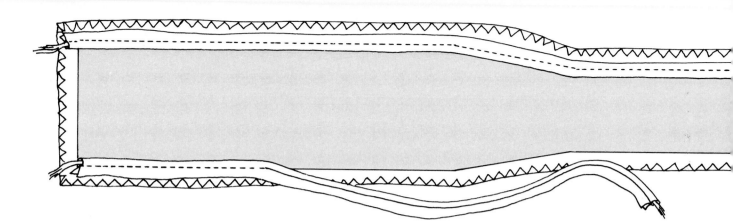

FINISHING

Materials:

Fine string for cording.
Lining material: linen, wool, cotton,
    crêpe, or a synthetic of medium weight.

1. With your sewing machine, run a row of stitches ½ inch beyond the needlepoint and trim away excess canvas. Do this for all three pieces.
2. Cut on the bias two strips 9½ inches long and two strips 40 inches long of lining material. With the right side of the material facing out, fold these pieces over the string and sew close to the string, using a zipper foot, to form cording.
3. Machine-sew the 40-inch pieces of cording along the long edges of the right side of the gusset (Fig. 4).
4. Sew the 9½-inch pieces to the top of the right sides of the front and back pieces (Fig. 5).

Fig. 5

USSET

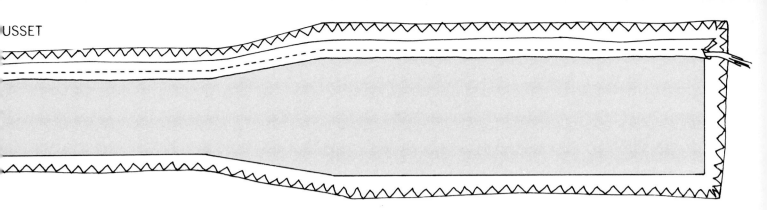

Fig. 4

5. Cut pieces of lining material to the size of each needle-point piece, adding ½ inch all around for seam allowance.

6. Pin one lining piece to one needlepoint side with both right sides facing in and machine-stitch around three sides very close to the edge of the outer row of needlepoint. Leave the bottom edge open for turning. Do this for the other side, turn the right sides out on both and steam lightly with an iron.

7. Sew the lining piece to the right side of the gusset along one edge only. Turn, steam, and sew the other side down by hand with invisible stitches.

8. Sew the open ends of the gusset together by hand, turning the raw edges in as you go.

9. Pin the front and back pieces to the gusset, centering the seam at the bottom carefully. Sew the front and back to the gusset by hand (Fig. 6).

Fig. 6

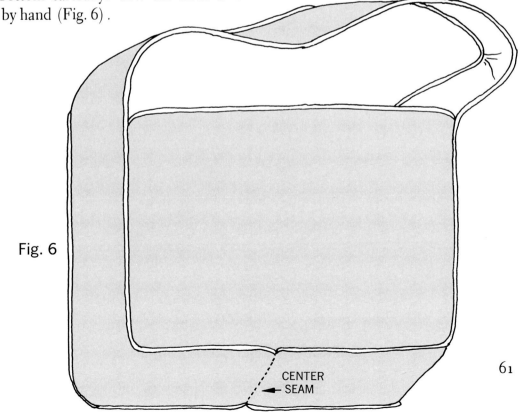

CENTER
← SEAM

61

STUFFED ANIMALS

The raccoon and the skunk can be either beanbags or stuffed animals, depending on whether you use beans or pillow stuffing. They are made in two pieces; the body is simple needlepoint. The knotted tufting stitch makes the fluffy tails.

INSTRUCTIONS FOR KNOTTED TUFTING

Use a full strand of three-thread yarn for #14 canvas. Start at the bottom right of the area to be covered.

1. Do not bring the needle from the back of the canvas, but begin by passing the needle into the first hole (A) from the front, holding down ½-inch of the wool with your left thumb. (Reverse this if you are left-handed.)
2. Bring the needle up from the hole on the diagonal upper left.
3. Pass the needle into the hole straight across two threads horizontally to the right.
4. Bring it up from the diagonal lower left hole, the one you began with. Pull taut.
5. Make a ½-inch-long loop and hold it down with your left thumb against the front of the canvas while you put the needle straight across two threads horizontally to

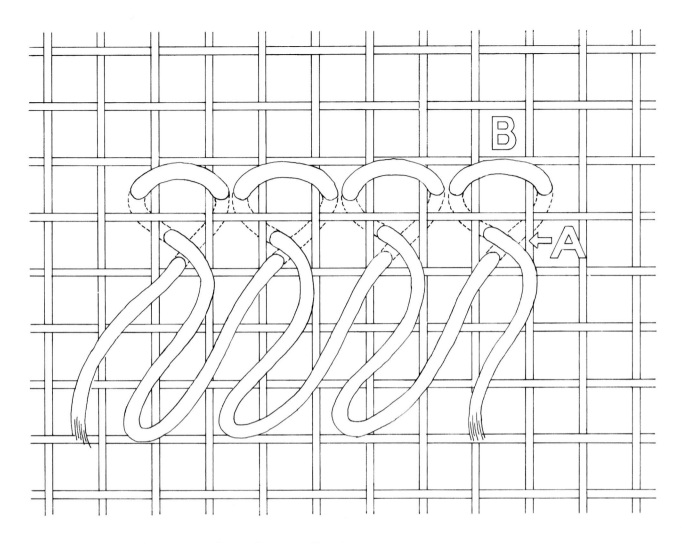

the left and repeat the process from Step 2. Continue
this way until you come to the end of the row.

End the row by cutting the wool to ½-inch after you draw
the wool to the front of the canvas, completing Step 4. Begin the next row at Point B in the diagram, directly above
the place where you started the first row. When the work is
completed, clip and trim the loops to form the fur.

(Plate 3)

Raccoon

(*Intermediate*)

#14 Canvas. Two threads of wool.

Work a random pattern of dots with dark brown along its back and legs, shading with medium gray brown to light gray brown toward the outer edges. The same dark brown is for the mask, with a little gray shading along the outer edges of the white in its face. The ears are outlined in white and shaded with medium and dark brown inside.

The rectangle marked off in bands is the pattern for the tail. Work the tail in alternate bands of beige and a medium brown that is different from the one used in the body.

Body:		Gray	4
Light gray brown	28		
Medium gray brown	28	*Tail:*	
Dark brown	8	Beige	9
White	4	Brown	10

(Plate 2)

Skunk

(*Easy*)

#14 Canvas. Two threads of wool.

The body is mostly black, with a white "V" on its back and a streak of white on its face. Use gray to outline the eyes, ears, and mouth. The tail has white markings and a

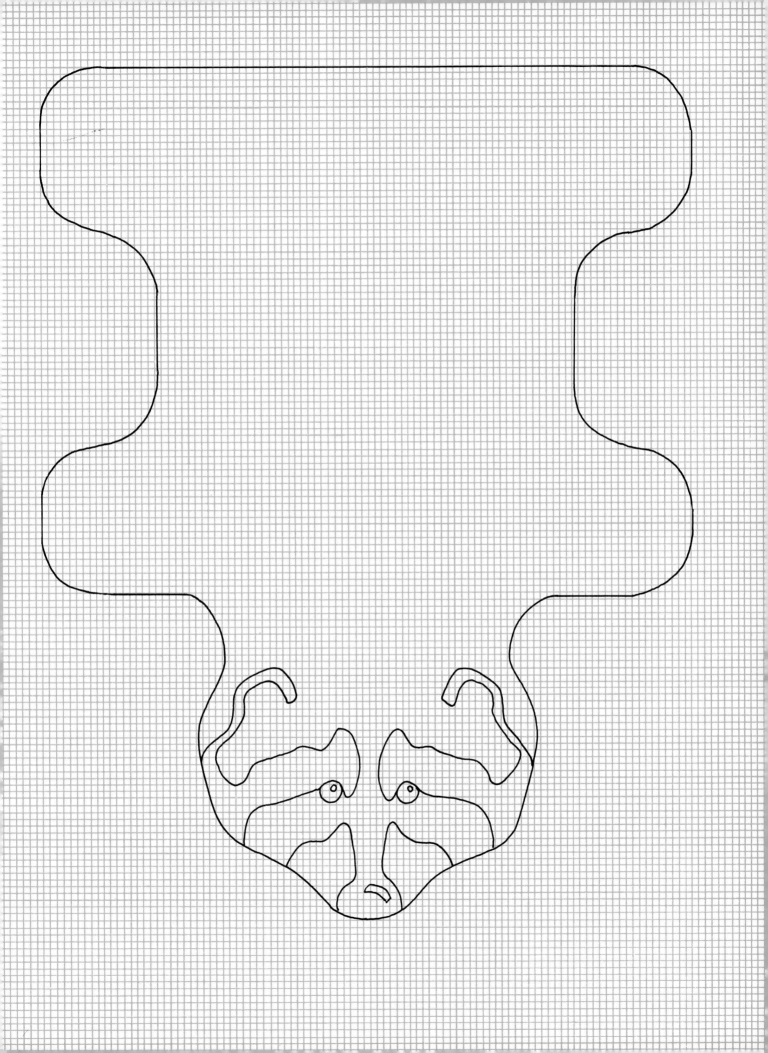

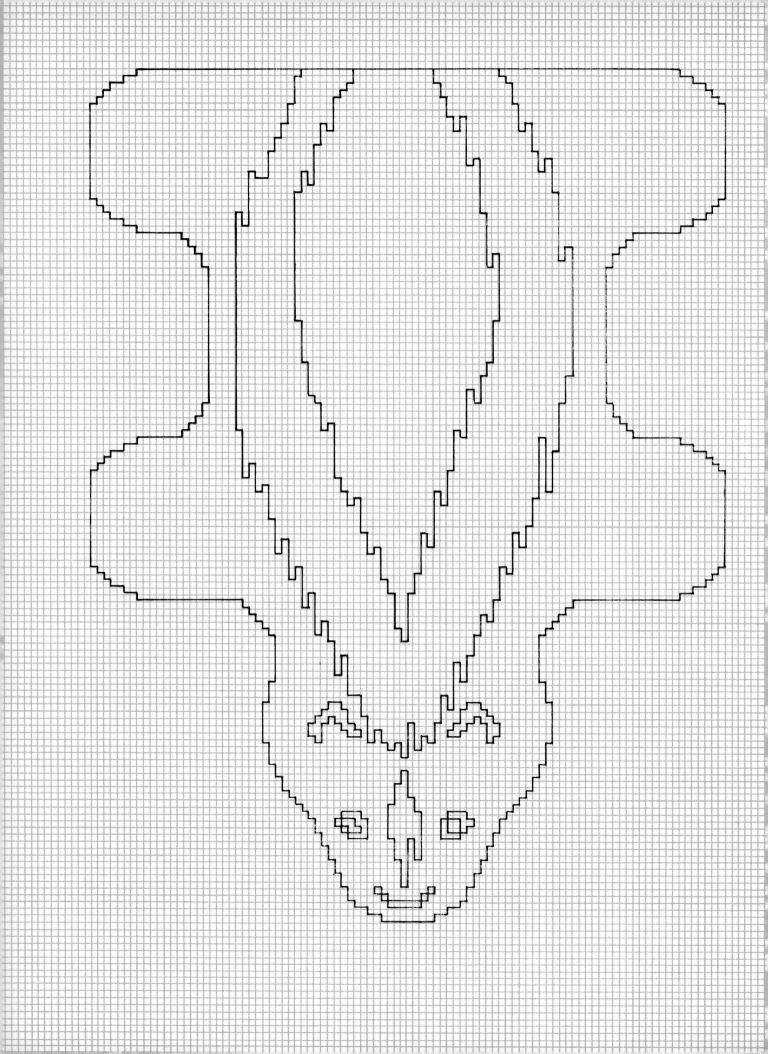

white tip, the rest is black. The wool count for the tail is included below.

$$\begin{array}{lr} \text{Black} & 50 \\ \text{Gray} & 1 \\ \text{White} & 35 \end{array}$$

FINISHING

Materials:
Lining: a heavy, tough material such as velvet or corduroy.
Stuffing: dacron, kapok, cotton, or beans.
Heavy button and carpet thread.

1. Run several rows of machine stitching ¼ inch from the edge of the worked area of both the body and the tail pieces. Trim away the excess canvas.
2. Cut a piece of lining material the same size and shape of the body only, including the ¼-inch seam allowance.
3. With their right sides together, sew the lining and the

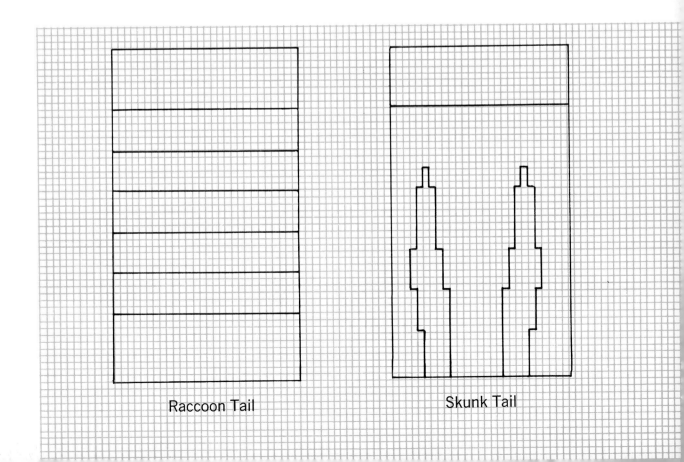

Raccoon Tail   Skunk Tail

needlepoint along the edge of the worked area, leaving the space between points A and B open (Fig. 1).

4. Turn this inside out, so that the right sides are facing out, and fill it with stuffing.

5. Fold the canvas edges on three sides of the tail piece to the wrong side and baste them down with heavy thread (Fig. 2).

6. Gather the short side of the tail that is basted down and pull it tightly to close (Fig. 3). Then, with the same threaded needle, sew the two side edges closed to form the finished tail.

7. Lay the open end of the tail in the center of the open seam of the body and sew it securely to the needlepoint with heavy thread (Fig. 4).

8. Invisibly sew the lining closed across the tail.

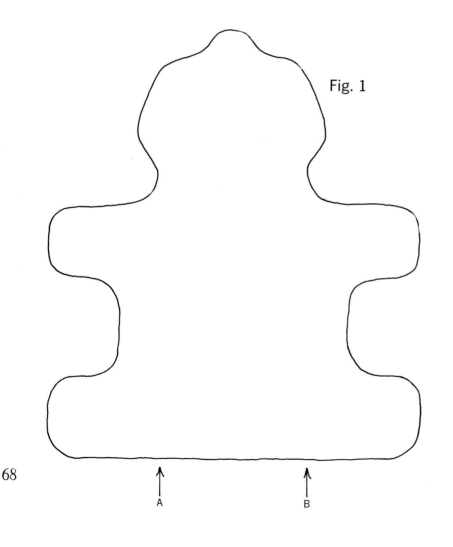

Fig. 1

A   B

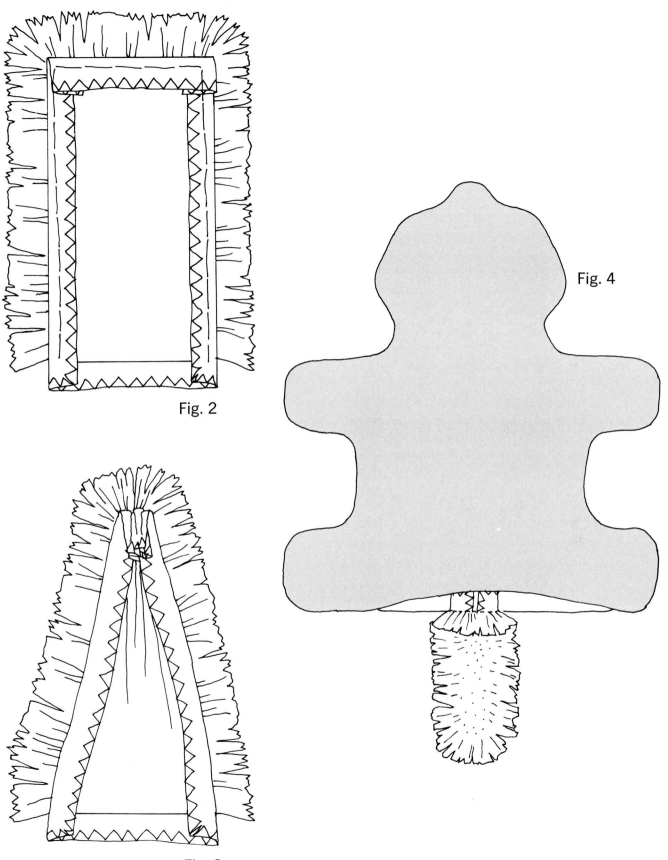

Fig. 2

Fig. 3

Fig. 4

BELTS

To take waist measurement, place your tape measure over the dress or pants for which the belt is to be worn. Don't judge by pant or skirt size. Cut the canvas 4 inches longer than this measurement to allow for any discrepancy. The designs are given as a 9-inch repeat, except the sandpipers, where the repeat is 6¾ inches. Mark the canvas center lightly with a pencil, then measure 9 inches in both directions as many times as necessary. Move the canvas along to trace the design, centering each section as you go according to the pencil lines.

To estimate the amount of wool you need, figure that it takes two and a half 33-inch strands of wool per inch — or seventy-five strands for a 30-inch belt.

(Plate 8)

Oriental Border

(Advanced)

#14 Canvas. Two threads of wool.

This design was taken from the border of a lovely old carpet whose colors have faded in streaks. Try to vary the colors subtly. I have chosen a variety of browns for the outlines of the shapes, and pale oranges and peach with several strong blues for accents. No two shapes are done in the same color combination. This is a good place for your creativity — and a good way to use up leftover pieces of wool.

Colors for the Oriental Belt:

- . Dark browns — outlines
- o Medium browns — inside the shapes
- ∕ Blues — accents
- x Oranges and peach — background

(Plate 2)

Butterflies

(Easy)

#14 Canvas. Two threads of wool.

Use bright colors against a bright background. Everything is done without shading except the grass, which has one darker green separating the blades.

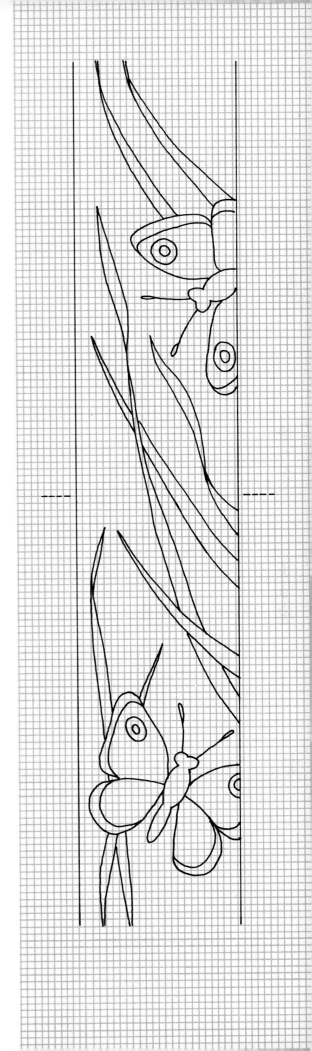

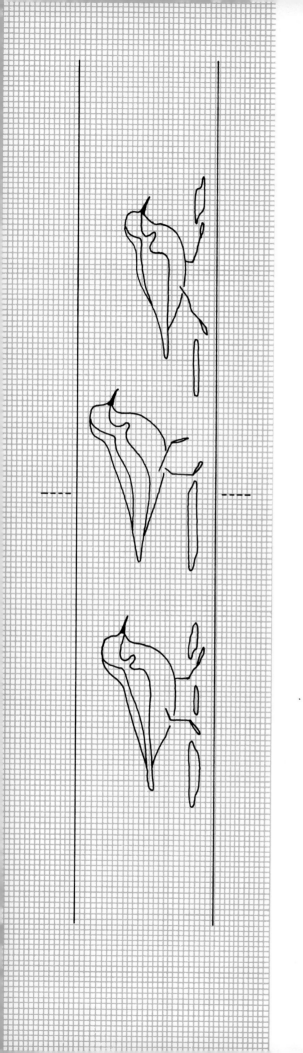

(Plate 4)

Sandpipers
(Easy)

#18 Canvas. Single thread of wool.

Measure 6¾ inches for the repeat. Use three shades of brown for the backs of the birds, and two shades of gray for their undersides. The background is sand color, with a darker shade of the same color for the shadows.

(Plate 12)

Art Nouveau
(Easy)

#14 Canvas. Two threads of wool.

The outline should be the darkest color you use. Pick a medium shade of another color for the background, and a light one to fill in the shapes. These shapes are more interesting if they aren't exactly alike, so vary them slightly.

FINISHING

Use belt buckles that clasp together so that you don't have to make eyelets (which are difficult to make and don't look very good in needlepoint anyway).

Materials:
   A buckle, which can be found in department stores, fabric

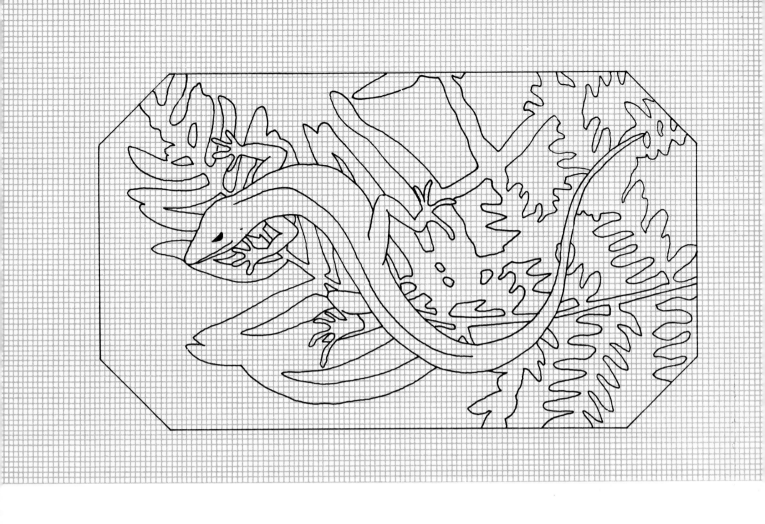

(Plate 12)

Chameleon

(Advanced)

#18 Canvas. Single thread of wool.

Use two slightly different greens that barely allow the lizard to be visible. The fun of this piece is in its ambiguity.

The yarn count is for one side only. Double the amounts if you want to repeat the design on the back. A plain back will take 18 strands of the background color.

Fern green, light	6	Yellow	1
Fern green, dark	3	Beige	2
Lizard green, light	1	Dark brown	1
Lizard green, dark	2	Background	11

The yarn count will cover both sides of the canvas.

Yellow   19
Orange   13
Pink   29

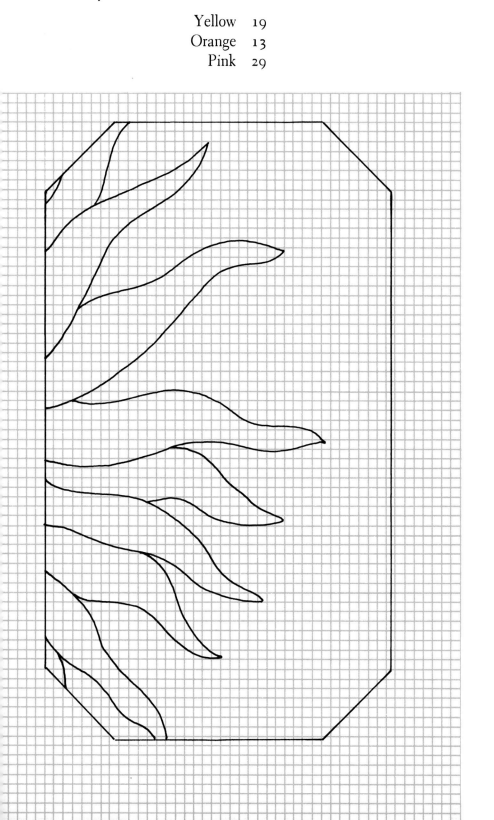

(Plate 2)

Sun

(Easy)

#10 Canvas. Full strand of three-thread wool.

EYEGLASS CASES

Needlepoint cases protect glasses efficiently and make excellent gifts. Initials on the backs of the cases — except for the sun design, which covers both sides — would add a nice personal touch.

(Plate 12)

Daisies

(Intermediate)

#14 Canvas. Two threads of wool.

The daisies may be worked in bright, primitive colors or subtly shaded.

The yarn count is for one side only. Double the amounts if you want to repeat the design on the back. A plain back will take 27 strands of background color.

White	7	Dark gray	1
Light green	2	Yellow	1
Medium green	1	Dark yellow	1
Dark green	1	Background	12
Light gray	1		

(Plate 8)

Lotus Blossom

(Easy)

#18 Canvas. Single thread of wool.

These lotus blossoms are taken from a miniature painting of women sitting by a pond, Rajput art, seventeenth century.

Light green	1
Medium green	1
Dark green	1
Light pink	1
Medium pink	1
Dark pink	1
Gold	2
Red	10
Background	8

FINISHING

Materials:
    String for cording.
    Interlining: buckram or pelon.
    Lining: any medium-weight fabric such
      as cotton, gabardine, silk, or satin.

1. Machine-stitch ⅜ inch from the worked area all around and trim away the excess canvas.
2. To make the cording, cut a piece of lining material on the bias, 1¼ inches x 14 inches. Fold it over the string, right sides out, and, using a zipper foot if you have one (or by hand) , sew closed.
3. Mark the center fold line on the canvas edge with a pencil. Sew the cording, by hand or machine, to the right side of the needlepoint, along the edge of one half as in Fig. 1. Then sew a piece of this cording on the opposite end between points A and B in the same figure.
4. Cut a piece of interlining ¼ inch smaller than the original outline to fit one half and lay it on the wrong side of the canvas, as shown in Fig. 2.
5. Turn the raw edges of the canvas and cording to the wrong side and baste down over the interlining.
6. Cut a piece of lining material ⅜ inch larger than the worked area. Pin it to the wrong side of the canvas, folding the seam allowance under. Sew it down by hand.
7. Fold it at the fold line you drew, right sides facing out. Sew one side, to point A, by hand, through all thicknesses, catching the needlepoint so that no canvas shows. Repeat this on the other side to point B.

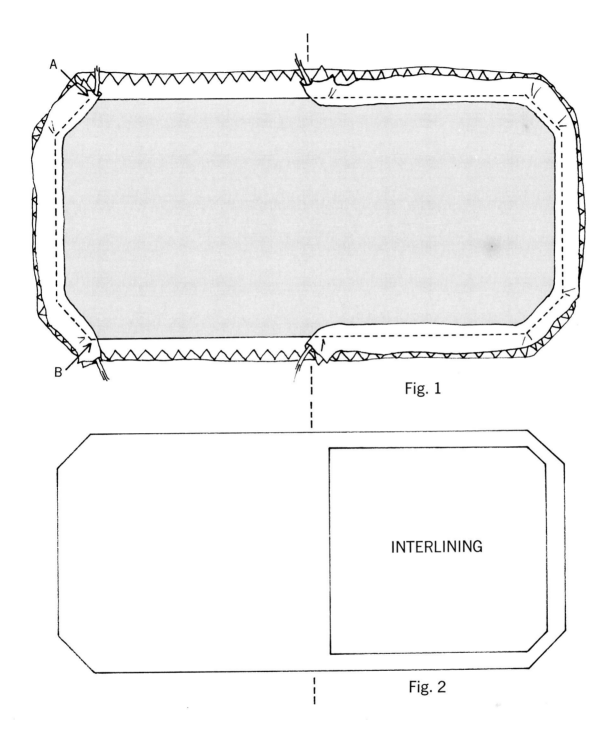

A

B

Fig. 1

INTERLINING

Fig. 2

79

Rouen Plate

(Advanced)

#18 Canvas. Single thread of wool.

This pattern is adapted from a plate made in the seventeenth century in the Rouen style.

Light blue	6	.
Dark blue	4	■
Background	14	

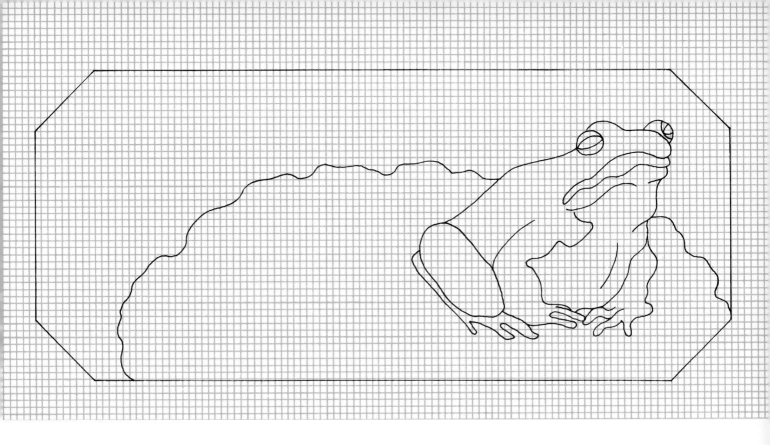

(Plate 2)

Frog on a Lily Pad

(Intermediate)

#14 Canvas. Two threads of wool.

Use two different greens for the frog and the lily pad.

White	2
Light gray	1
Dark gray	1
Light yellow green	2
Medium yellow green	2
Dark yellow green	1
Darkest yellow green	1
Orange	1
Light green	8
Medium green	4
Background	12

CREDIT CARD CASES

Here is an elegant way to keep credit cards within easy reach.

(Plate 5)

Shell

(Easy)

#14 Canvas. Two threads of wool.

This is a simple scallop folded in half.

Light pink	9
Medium pink	4
Dark pink	2
Background	16

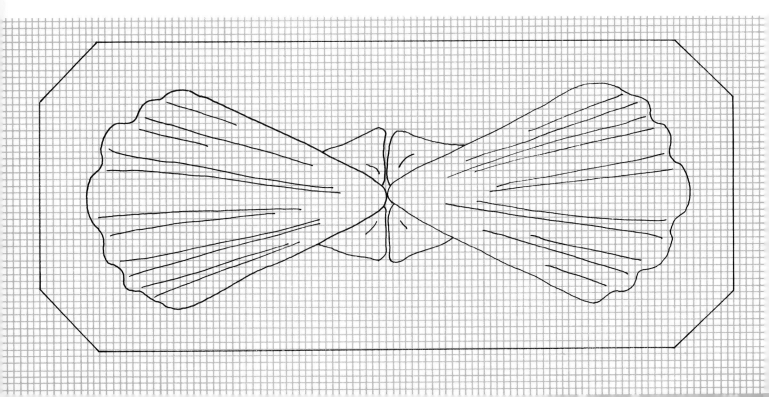

shops, leather supply stores, and, often, needlepoint shops.

Lining material: any medium-weight fabric will do, but grosgrain ribbon is convenient and wears well.

1. Run several rows of machine stitching on the canvas border ½ inch from the worked area on all sides. Trim away the excess canvas.

2. Turn under the canvas on the long sides to the wrong side and baste down by hand, leaving the buckle ends open.

3. Pull the raw edges of the canvas through the buckle on each side, overlapping 1 inch. Pin and adjust to the waist size, then sew down firmly by hand.

4. Sew the lining to the back, turning the edges and pulling as you go, so the lining is slightly shorter than the needlepoint. This will prevent the lining from puckering when the belt is curved around a waist. To keep it from being too bulky at the ends, join the turned edge of the lining to the end of the worked area without overlapping.

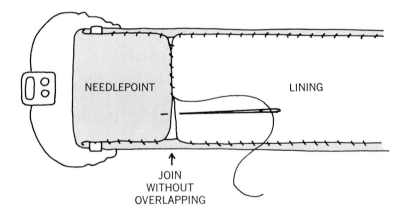

NEEDLEPOINT   LINING

↑
JOIN
WITHOUT
OVERLAPPING

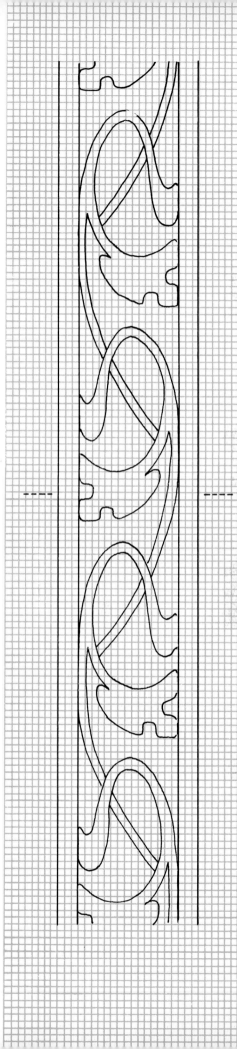

(Plate 4)

Sandpipers

(Easy)

18 Canvas. Single thread of wool.

The yarn count is for one side only. Double the amounts
if you want to repeat the design on the back. A plain back
will take 18 strands of the background color you prefer,
sand or blue.

Light brown	1	Dark gray	1
Medium brown	1	Sand	12
Dark brown	1	Dark sand	1
Light gray	1	Blue	4

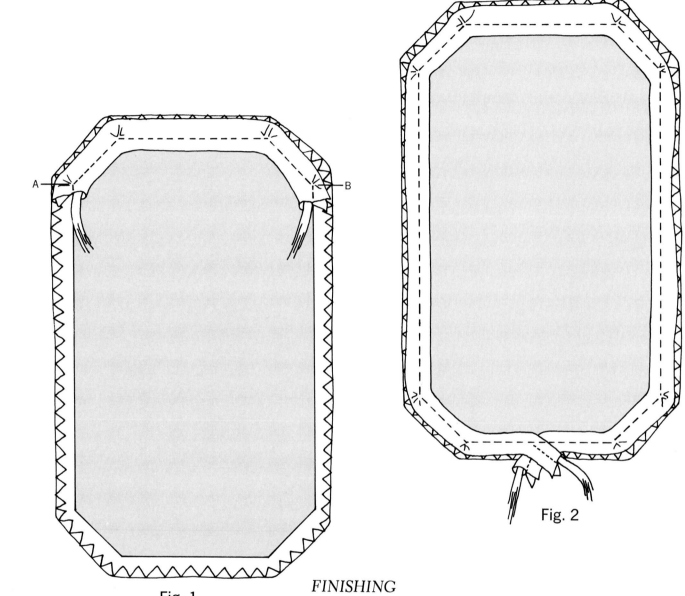

Fig. 1

Fig. 2

FINISHING

Materials:

Lining material: medium-weight fabric such as silk, cotton, faille, or grosgrain. Don't use satin, it's too slippery.

Interlining: either pelon or buckram. (This isn't necessary if the needlepoint is worked on #10 canvas.)
String for cording.

1. Cut a strip of lining material on the bias, 1 inch x 23 inches. With the zipper foot of your machine (or by hand) sew it, right sides out, over the string to make the cording.
2. Run several rows of machine stitching ½ inch from the worked area of your needlepoint. Trim away the excess canvas.
3. If you have worked only one side in needlepoint, cut a piece of lining material ½ inch bigger than the original outline to use as a back.
4. Sew a piece of cording to the right side of the top of the back between points A and B (Fig. 1), and a piece around the entire edge of the front (Fig. 2).
5. Cut two pieces of interlining ¼ inch smaller than the original outline all around. Lay one of these on the wrong side of each piece.
6. Turn the raw edges of the canvas and cording to the wrong sides of both pieces and baste down over the interlining.
7. Cut two pieces of lining material ½ inch bigger than the original outlines. Sew these to the wrong sides of both pieces with invisible stitches, tucking under all seam allowances as you go.
8. Hold the two pieces with their lining sides together and sew through the cording and the needlepoint of both sides between points A and B (Fig. 1). Go over the stitches at points A and B to reinforce the stress points.

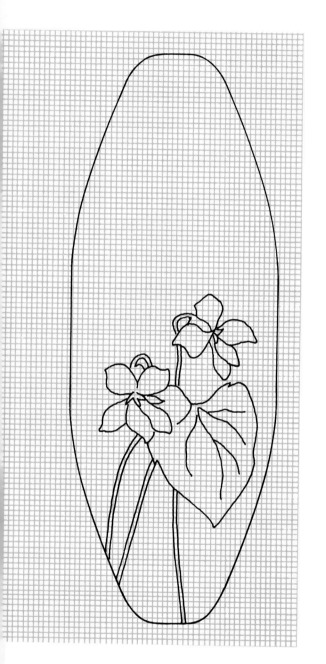

EMBROIDERY SCISSORS CASES

If you have a favorite pair of embroidery scissors, this might be one of your first projects. The case is designed for scissors 3½ inches long, a standard size. If yours are bigger, just add a few rows on all sides when you work the needlepoint.

(Plate 7)

Violets

(Intermediate)

#18 Canvas. Single thread of wool.

This dainty pattern deserves soft colors and delicate shading. Notice the blue in the flowers and the pale blue used to highlight the leaves. Take your time with the shading.

Light yellow green	1	Medium purple	1
Light blue	1	Dark purple	1
Light green	1	Darkest purple	1
Dark green	1	Medium blue	1
Darkest green	1	Background	14
Light purple	1		

(Plate 12)

Oriental Border

(Easy)

#14 Canvas. Two threads of wool.

This graph has an easy count and is fun to work.

Red	2	·
Dark blue	3	╱
Green	2	╲
Light blue	5	×
Background	13	

FINISHING

Materials:

Lining: a light-weight fabric such as silk, satin, or cotton.

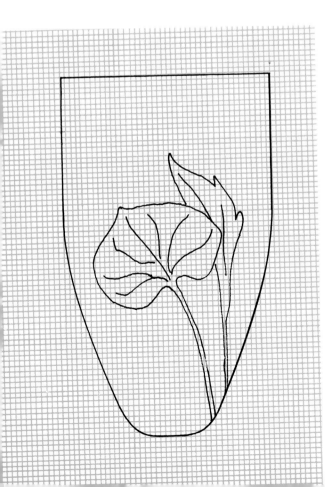

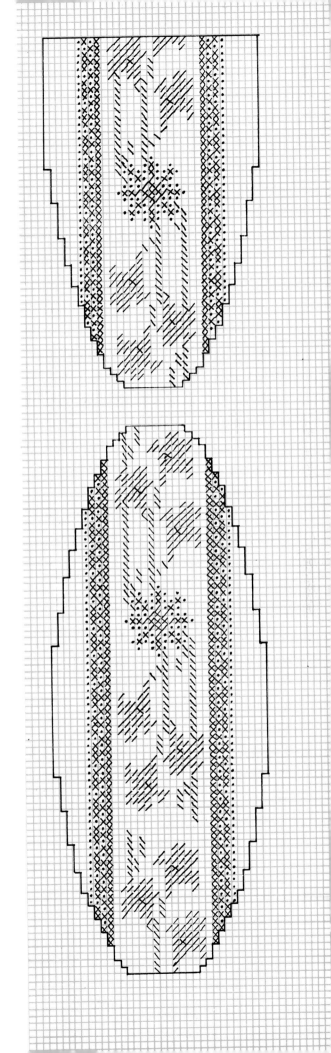

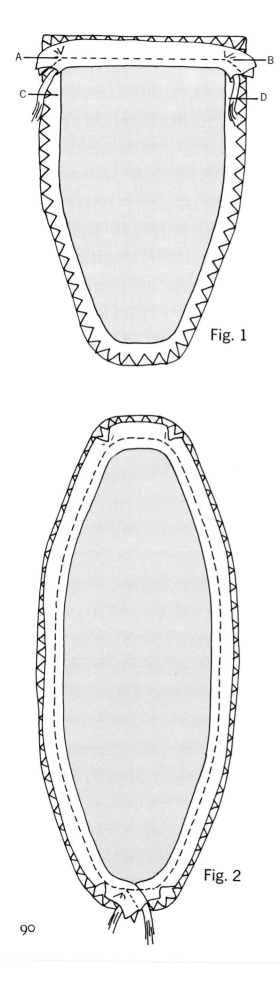

Fig. 1

Fig. 2

String for cording.
Grosgrain ribbon, ¼ inch wide. (This is
   optional.)

1. Cut a strip of lining material on the bias, 1 inch x 17
   inches. With the zipper foot of your machine (or by
   hand) sew it, right sides out, over the string to make the
   cording.
2. Run several rows of machine stitching ¼ inch from
   the worked area of both pieces. Trim away the excess
   canvas.
3. Sew a piece of the cording to the right side of the top
   of the back between points A and B (Fig. 1), and a piece
   around the entire edge of the front (Fig. 2).
4. Turn the raw edges of the canvas and cording to the
   wrong sides of both pieces and baste down.
5. To make the flap loop, cut a piece of grosgrain ribbon
   3 inches long or cut a piece of lining material ¾ inch
   x 3 inches; fold it lengthwise, right sides out. Then fold
   the raw edges under and sew them together invisibly by
   hand, forming a ¼-inch tube. Sew the ribbon or
   lining material to the back ½ inch from the top edge
   between points C and D of Fig. 1.
6. Cut two pieces of lining material ¼ inch bigger than
   the original outlines. Sew these to the wrong sides of
   both pieces with invisible stitches, tucking under all
   seam allowances as you go.
7. Hold the two pieces with their lining sides together and
   sew them together through the cording and the needlepoint of both sides between points A and B (Fig. 1).
   Go over the stitches at points A and B to reinforce the
   stress points.

CHANGE PURSES

These are very useful and quick to do. You might consider doing a plain one with initials on one side.

(Plate 9)

Tea Rose

(Intermediate)

#14 Canvas. Two threads of wool.

This is an abstraction of a photograph from *Audubon* magazine. The gray areas on the drawing indicate background. Use vivid colors.

Chartreuse	4	Gold	1
Light green	4	Light pink	1
Dark green	4	Medium pink	3
Light yellow	1	Dark pink	1
Medium yellow	1	Background	4

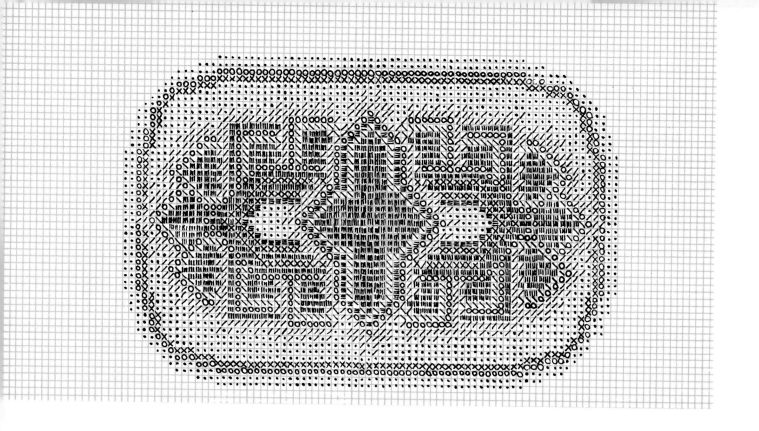

(Plate 6)

Persian Carpet

(Easy)

#14 Canvas. Two threads of wool.

This design was inspired by a Moghul carpet made in the early 1600's.

White	1	ⅲ
Light blue	2	x
Red	6	.
Yellow	4	∘
Orange	7	≡
Green	5	∕
Navy	2	∖

FINISHING

Materials:

4-inch zipper, or a longer one of nylon
   which you can sew across at 4 inches and
   cut away excess.
Lining: medium-weight fabric, such as
   cotton or silk.

1. Run several rows of machine stitching ⅜ inch from
   the worked area all around. Trim away excess canvas.
2. With right sides together, sew lining and needlepoint along the edges between Points A and B and
   between C and D. Turn right sides out (Fig. 1).
3. Fold it in half and sew the edges together between
   A and B and on the other side between C and D
   (Fig. 2).
4. Baste the zipper to the needlepoint and sew it down
   by hand with small stitches. Sew the lining to the
   zipper on the inside.

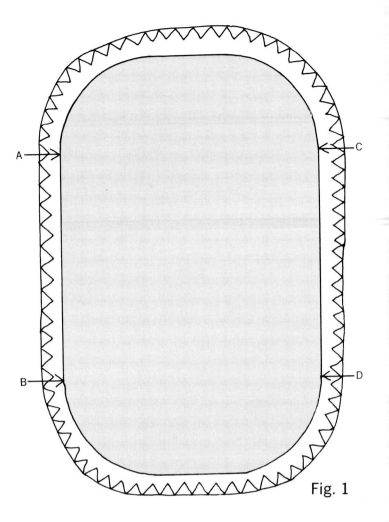

Fig. 1

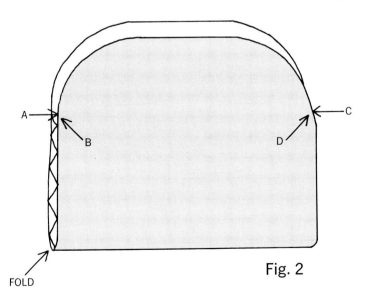

FOLD

Fig. 2

PICTURE FRAMES

These needlepoint frames are destined to become heir-looms. They are admittedly a production to mount but well worth your patience. Work four extra rows on the inner and outer edges of all frames for turning. The openings are for standard-size snapshots, but you could put small mir-rors in them instead.

(Plate 4)

Sandpipers
(Easy)

#18 Canvas. Single thread of wool.

The opening of this frame is for Polaroid snapshots, 3½ inches x 4 inches. Don't forget to work four extra rows all around.

Light brown	1
Medium brown	1
Dark brown	1
Light gray	1
Dark gray	1
Sand	20
Dark sand	1
Blue	27

(Plate 7)

Art Nouveau Pansies
(Easy)
14 Canvas. Two threads of wool.

Orange	2
Pink	4
Lavender	5
Mauve	4
Dark blue	7
Light green	2
Dark green	2

Backgrounds:

Light	35
Medium	25

(Plate 8)

Oriental

(*Intermediate*)

#10 Canvas. Full strand of three-thread wool.

This design is taken from the border of a Derbend rug from North Caucasia. If you want to make this an even richer looking piece, you can vary the colors. For example, you could use a slightly darker blue mixed with the light blue in streaks.

Light blue	29	x
Dark blue	39	/
White	5	‖‖
Light yellow	5	o
Dark yellow	2	⊙
Red	24	·
Brown	3	≡

(Plate 5)

Shells

(Advanced)

#18 Canvas. One thread of wool.

This graceful frame should be attempted only by someone who has the patience and experience to shade these shells carefully. If you would like to use references for color, these can be found in the Golden Nature Guide series on shells. They are, beginning with the top, from left to right: Gold-Ringer, Folded Scallop, and Grooved-Toothed Cowrie. Bottom: Bednall's Volute, Junonia Volute, Leopard Scallop, Aulicus Cone, and Angular Volute.

Take the photograph in this book or your reference to the place where you will buy your wool and pick the colors you want for the shells. You also will need:

> Green 3
> Background 35

FINISHING

Materials:

Cardboard, mat, or illustration board, medium weight — available at art supply stores and some stationers'.

Exacto or mat knife, for cutting cardboard.

Backing: any heavy fabric, such as velvet, corduroy, faille, or wool.

Bias binding: the same color as the inner edge of the needlepoint.

Wrapping paper: plain brown variety or something fancy that looks nice with the design of your frame.

Heavy button and carpet thread.

Glue. The real key to making frames is very strong glue of the rubber cement type. Art supply stores carry "one coat" rubber cement, which is extra-strong. The best kind is "Craftsman Cement," available at Tandy Leather Stores. When it is time to glue, coat both surfaces to be joined, let them dry until they're tacky, line them up carefully, and press together.

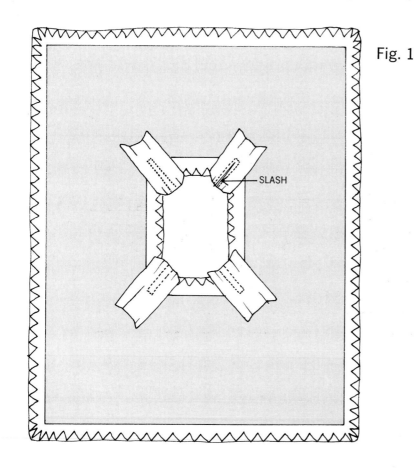

Fig. 1

SLASH

1. To make the front half of the frame, cut a piece of cardboard the size of the frame. Cut a hole in the center, according to the outline. Using the cardboard piece as a guide, cut a piece of wrapping paper ¼ inch smaller on the outside and center-opening edges (which makes the center hole larger).

2. Run several rows of machine stitching ½ inch from the inner and outer edges on the raw canvas. Trim away excess canvas.

3. Cut four pieces of bias tape 2 inches long. Place one on each corner of the right side of the needlepoint on the diagonal. Stitch through the four extra rows of needlepoint to the corner, leaving about ⅛ inch between two rows of machine stitching, something like an open-ended button hole. Go over this several times with tiny stitches. Slash to the corners through the tape reinforcement. (Fig. 1)

4. Place the cardboard on the wrong side of the needlepoint, turn the tape on the inner corners to the back. With heavy thread and long stitches, lace the needle-

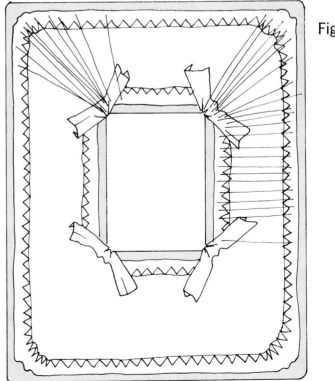

Fig. 2

point evenly over the cardboard. Lace the four corners first, then lace the sides into place. You will need to use many long stitches to make the needlepoint smooth on the front. (Fig. 2)

5. Glue the paper to the cardboard, covering the threads and raw edges.

6. To make the easel for the back of the frame, cut a piece of cardboard according to Fig. 3. Cut a piece of backing material according to Fig. 4. Clip where indicated. Glue the cardboard easel to the backing (Fig. 5). Turn the edges to the back and glue to the cardboard. Cut a piece of wrapping paper according to the pattern in

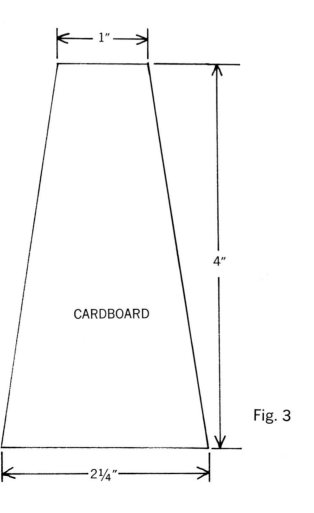

Fig. 3

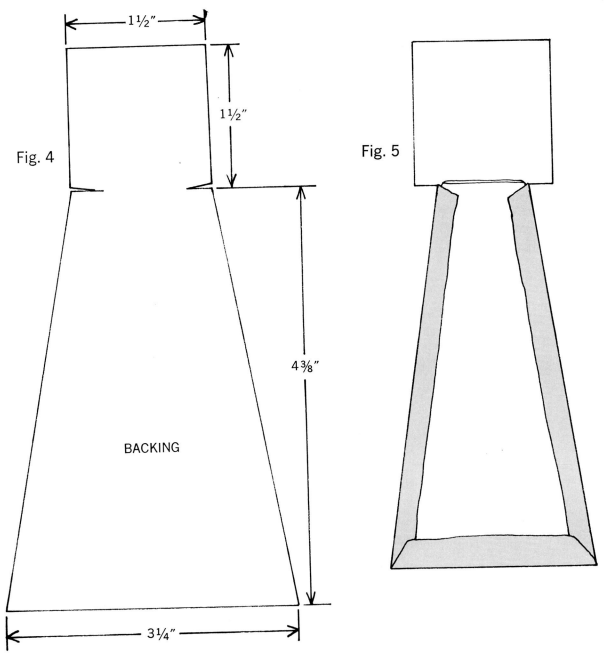

1½″

1½″

Fig. 4

4⅜″

BACKING

3¼″

Fig. 5

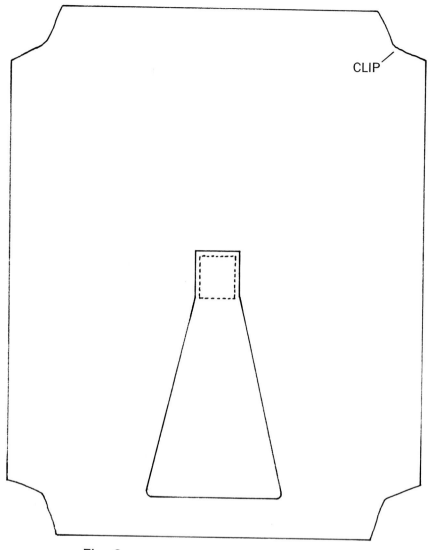

CLIP

Fig. 6

Fig. 3 and glue to the back of the easel, covering the raw edges.

7. To make the back half of the frame, cut another piece of cardboard the size of the frame. Then cut a piece of backing 1 inch bigger all around than the cardboard. Turn under the edges of the fabric top of the easel and sew it to the backing, centered, and making sure that the bottom of the easel measures 1 inch up from the bottom of the frame. (Fig. 6)

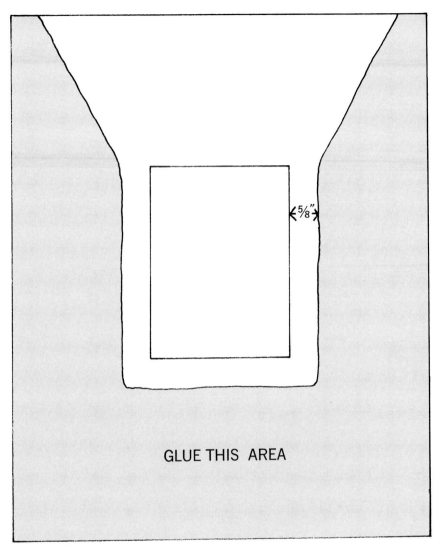

5/8"

GLUE THIS AREA

Fig. 7

8. Glue the cardboard to the backing to which the easel
   has been attached. Clip the corners, turn and glue the
   edges to the other side of the cardboard. Cut another
   piece of wrapping paper, as in Step #1. Glue it to the
   cardboard, covering the raw edges.
9. Coat the two paper sides with glue as in Fig. 7 (do not
   glue top section). When the glue is tacky (see under
   Materials), press the two halves of the frame together.
   The photograph can be slipped in at the top.